Disney · PIXAR

TOY STORY 4

Level 5

Re-told by: Mo Sanders

Series Editor: Rachel Wilson

Contents

In This Book

Woody

A sheriff doll and one of Bonnie's toys

Buzz Lightyear

A space ranger toy and Woody's best friend

Bonnie

A little girl who loves her toys but is worried about starting school

Forky

A strange little toy who Bonnie makes from trash in her kindergarten class

Gabby Gabby

A doll who lives in an antique store

Bo Peep

An old friend of Woody's who became a lost toy

Before You Read

Introduction

Woody only wants his kid to be happy. For Bonnie, that means spending time with her new toy, Forky. So, when Forky runs away on a family vacation, Woody goes to bring him back. But there are terrible dangers, big surprises, old friends, and a doll who wants to take his voice. Can Woody return to Bonnie and all his friends? Or will he become a lost toy?

. . . .

Activities

1 **What do you think? Answer the questions with the character names.**

1 Who is the new toy?

2 Who does Woody meet in the antique store?

3 Which old friend does Woody meet again?

a Gabby Gabby

b Bo Peep

c Forky

2 **What do you think? What is the worst thing for a toy?**

1 You're in a house but your kid never plays with you.

2 You're in a store but no person buys you.

3 You're a lost toy.

1   The New Toy

Once, Woody was his kid's favorite toy. But Andy grew up and went to college, and now the sheriff doll was one of Bonnie's toys. Life was very different here. Woody wasn't one of Bonnie's favorites. She often left him in the cupboard during games.

His friend Buzz tried to make him feel better. "Are you all right, Woody? She'll choose you next time," he said. But Woody wasn't so sure.

One morning, Bonnie's dad said, "Bonnie, it's time to go. We're meeting your new teachers." It was time for Bonnie to see her kindergarten class for the first time.

Bonnie was very quiet and Woody was worried about her. He saw her backpack on the bedroom floor and he had an idea.

"I'm going to kindergarten with her!" he decided. He ran and jumped into the backpack. Bonnie's mom drove them to the kindergarten.

At kindergarten, the kids began to make things, but Bonnie's crayons fell in the trash. Quickly, Woody pulled everything out of the trash. Bonnie didn't see him, but she saw the trash. She glued some eyes on a plastic fork. Then she gave it a mouth, arms, and feet.

Later, she showed the strange figure to her parents. "His name is Forky!" she cried.

Woody got a surprise on the way home—Forky sat up and looked around!

Back home, the other toys met Forky. But there was a problem. Forky wanted only one thing—to jump in the trash!

"Uh … why?" a toy asked.

"Because he's made of trash," explained Woody. "But believe me—Forky is THE most important toy to Bonnie right now."

Forky ran for the trash again. Woody stopped him, and he had to stop him the next time.

And the next time …

And the time after that …

2 A Family Vacation

The next day, the family went for a short vacation in an RV. Woody still had to stop Forky jumping in the trash. But Woody couldn't watch him all the time. When Bonnie was asleep, Forky climbed to an open window.

"I am not a toy!" he shouted. "I'm trash!" And then he jumped out the window of the RV!

Woody jumped up. He had to get Forky back. "I'll meet you at the RV park," he cried bravely, and he jumped out the window, too.

Woody found Forky next to the road. They started the long walk to the RV park where Bonnie's family was staying.

"Why do I have to be a toy?" Forky asked.

Woody tried to explain. "You're Bonnie's toy. You have to be there for her. That's your job—when she's with you, Bonnie feels happy and warm."

At last, Forky understood. He always felt happy and warm when he was in the trash. "I'm Bonnie's trash! Woody, we have to go! She needs me!"

Soon they were in the town, near the RV park. Woody could see the park, but suddenly he stopped. He was outside an antique store and there was something in the store window …

It was a lamp that he knew very well. When he was Andy's toy years ago, that lamp sat in the room of Andy's sister. A figure called Bo Peep and her three little sheep stood at that lamp.

"Bo?" said Woody quietly.

3 The Antique Store

"Woody? said Forky. "Aren't we going to Bonnie?"

"Yes," said Woody, "but my old friend could be in there ... Come on."

They climbed in. The store was closed and it was dark and quiet. "Bo?" called Woody.

Suddenly, there was a noise. "Is that Bo?" asked Forky.

No—it was a tall doll who didn't speak. There was a girl doll, too. "My name's Gabby Gabby," she said. "It's nice to meet you."

"Are you two lost?" asked Gabby Gabby.

"No, no," said Woody, "but we are looking for a lost toy. Her name's Bo Peep."

Gabby Gabby smiled. "Bo Peep? I know Bo. We'll take you to her."

"Well … okay," said Woody. There was something strange about this place, but he wanted to see his friend again.

Gabby Gabby looked at Woody. "You have a voice box," she said. "I have one, too, but mine doesn't work."

"The store's opening soon," said Gabby Gabby.

Woody saw the light outside. "We can't stay," he said.
Something was not right here.

"You can't leave yet," said Gabby Gabby. "You have what I
need." She pointed at Woody's chest. "Right … inside … there."

His voice box! There were more tall dolls around Woody now.

Suddenly, the door opened. A woman came in with her
granddaughter. Quickly, Woody ran out and pulled the string
on his back.

The girl picked up Woody. "Grandma, I found this on the floor!" she said. "Can I take it to the park?"

"Sure," said Grandma. It was her store and people didn't usually buy the toys.

The girl carried Woody outside. He looked back at the store. Forky was still in there! At the park, Woody waited for the right time. He had to go back and get Forky! As soon as he could, he started to run.

4 Old Friends

There were a lot of kids at the park and a lot of toys. Wait! Woody couldn't believe it—he knew one of those toys. It was his old friend, Bo Peep!

"It's you!" Bo cried happily. Woody pointed at all the children. "So, which kid is yours?"

"None," said Bo. She was a lost toy now. She and her friends traveled from place to place. They never stayed with any one kid. It was a life that Bo loved.

Bo asked Woody to come to a children's party.

"I can't," said Woody. "I have to get back to my kid." Woody explained about Forky and the antique store.

"We know that store," said Bo. "We were there for years."

"Will you help me?" asked Woody.

Bo looked at her old friend. "All right," she agreed.

Woody followed Bo and her friends to the store. They were nearly there when he saw another friendly face—Buzz! He was there to find Woody and Forky.

Inside the store, Bo pointed to a high cupboard. "Your friend's up there."

"That's a big jump," said Buzz.

Bo smiled. "We know the right toy to help."

Suddenly, the store door opened. Bonnie and her mom walked in! "It's Bonnie!" cried Woody excitedly. "We have to get Forky now!"

Bo pulled him back. "What are you doing? You need to follow the plan!"

Seconds later the door opened again, and Bonnie and her mom left. Woody could only watch.

5 The Plan to Save Forky

Bo took Woody to meet one of her friends, a doll with a motorbike. His name was Duke Caboom.

"We need your help," Bo said. She wanted Duke to take Woody on his motorbike and jump up to Gabby Gabby's cupboard. At first Duke said no because he always crashed.

"We *need* a toy who can crash onto the cupboard," said Bo.

"Crash?" said Duke.

"Yes," said Bo. "You are the only one who can crash the way you do!"

Duke was ready. It was time for the big jump. Duke's motorbike went up, up, up …

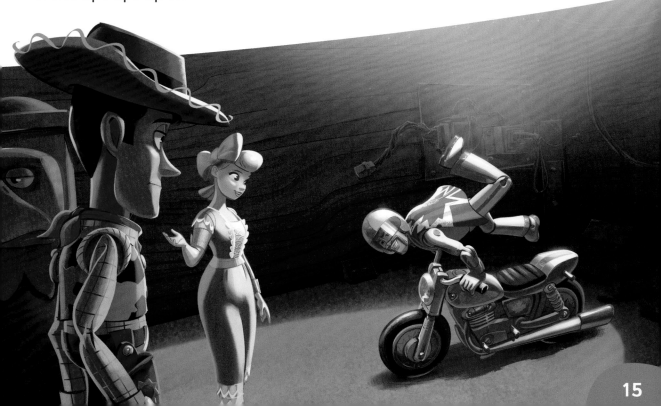

Then it crashed down. Woody fell onto the store's cat! Gabby Gabby's tall dolls started to run at them.

"Duke! Get us out of here!" shouted Bo.

She and the other toys held the string behind his motorbike. Woody tried not to fall off the angry cat. Seconds later, they were outside …

"Forky's still in there," Woody said.

"Woody, it's better to wait," Buzz tried to explain. "I saw it … Bonnie's backpack!" But Woody didn't listen. He started to walk back inside.

"Open your eyes, Woody," Bo said softly. "There are a lot of kids out there. You can't just think about one all the time."

"I have to look after Bonnie," answered Woody. "A lost toy can't understand that!"

"I'm not the one who's lost." Bo walked away sadly with her friends.

Woody looked at Buzz. "I don't leave toys behind," he said.

"Woody …" Buzz began, but his friend went back inside. Buzz turned to go back to the RV park.

6 Gabby Gabby and her Kid

Back in the antique store, Woody was afraid. He was also ready to fight, but Gabby Gabby only wanted to talk.

"How nice for you. You had kids to play with you," she said sadly. "Was it wonderful?"

Woody felt sorry for her. She only wanted to have a kid, too, but her voice box didn't work.

"Okay," he said, "you can have my voice box. Just let me have Forky."

Back in the RV, Buzz explained everything. "We need to get Woody and Forky from the antique store."

"How do we do that?" asked a toy.

There was another problem—Bonnie's dad started to drive the RV away! "It's okay," said Buzz. "Bonnie left her backpack at the store. We'll go back for it."

But Bonnie didn't remember the backpack. Buzz had to think fast. "Your backpack's in the ANTIQUE store!" he shouted.

Bonnie looked up. "Oh, no, my backpack!"

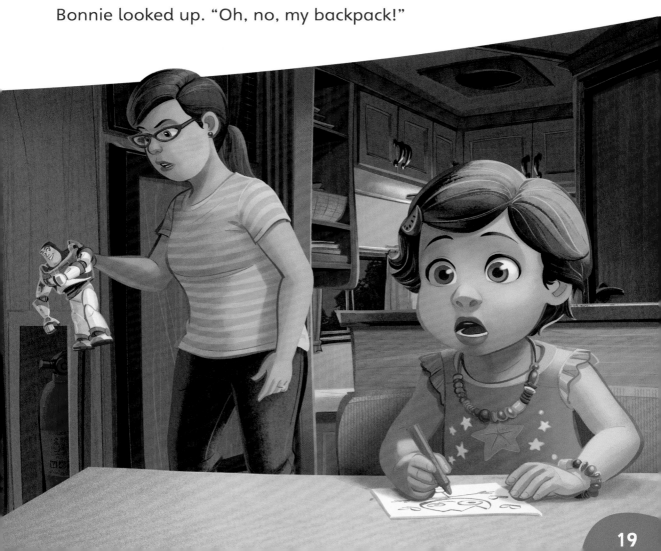

At the store, Woody woke up. He had no voice box, but Forky was with him. He heard a voice. "Hi, we called about the backpack?" It was Bonnie's mom!

"Oh, yes," said the woman from the store. "Please have a look for it."

Woody saw it now—Bonnie's backpack! "Quick!" he said to Forky. They ran and jumped inside.

From the backpack, they could see Gabby Gabby near the girl from the store. The girl picked up Gabby Gabby and pulled the string on her back.

"I'm Gabby Gabby and I love you," she said with her new voice box—Woody's voice box!

"You can take that doll home," the girl's grandmother said.

"This is it," Woody thought. "Gabby Gabby's going to get her kid at last!"

But then the girl just said, "No!" She threw Gabby Gabby into an old box and ran outside.

Woody heard another voice—Bonnie! "There's my backpack!"

He turned to Forky. "Listen. Tell Buzz to get the RV to the carnival. Meet us at the carousel." Then he ran out of the backpack before Bonnie saw him.

7 Duke Caboom Rides Again

After Bonnie left, Woody ran to Gabby Gabby. "You can have your voice box back," the doll said quietly. "I don't need it now."

"Yes, you do!" Woody said. "There are a lot of kids out there. One of them is Bonnie. You can be her toy!"

"He's right," said a voice from behind them. It was Bo! Bo smiled and held out her hand to Gabby Gabby. "Come on."

In the RV, Forky explained Woody's plan. But how could they get the RV to the carousel? The toys thought fast. They turned off the GPS and hid.

"*Turn left here*," said one of the toys. "*Take the next right*." Dad always listened to the GPS so he turned the wheel.

Woody, Bo, and their friends were at the highest place in the carnival. But could they get to the carousel in time? Bo had an idea—Duke had to jump to it with a string. Then the other toys could climb along the string. But Duke was afraid. He didn't want to crash.

"You've got this, Duke," said Bo.

"You're right. I'm DUKE CABOOM!"

He was ready. His motorbike went faster and faster, and then it was in the air, high above the carnival. Seconds later, he crashed. Yes! The other toys could climb along the long string. From here, it wasn't far to the carousel.

It was nearly time for the RV to be there, too. "Come on," said Bo. But Gabby Gabby didn't come …

The doll could see a little girl at the carnival.

"She's crying," said Gabby Gabby. "I think she's lost …"

Woody understood. "Are you sure?" he asked.

"Yes." Gabby Gabby wanted this girl, not Bonnie, to be her kid.

Woody smiled. "We're changing the plan," he told Bo.

The doll moved closer and the little girl saw her. She picked Gabby Gabby up. "Are … are you lost, too?" the girl asked.

The girl pulled the string on Gabby Gabby's back. "I'm Gabby Gabby," said the doll. "Will you be my friend?"

The girl stopped crying and held the doll to her chest. A minute later, a police officer saw the girl and her new doll. "It's okay," said the police officer. "We'll help you find your parents."

Woody and Bo watched and they knew—at last, Gabby Gabby had her kid. Now they had to get to the carousel.

8 New Beginnings

The other toys were already there, on top of the RV.

Woody looked at Bo Peep. "Goodbye," he said sadly. He walked slowly along the top of the RV. Buzz stood in his way.

"She'll be okay," Buzz said. "I mean, Bonnie will be okay. She has Forky back and she has us."

Woody understood—Bonnie had Forky and all the other toys. But Woody needed to be with Bo Peep. He loved her. It was time to say goodbye to all his old friends.

The RV started to drive away. Woody and Bo watched from the top of the carousel. Woody smiled. It was the start of an exciting new life together.

Inside the RV, the other toys watched their old friend through the back window. "Does this mean that Woody's a lost toy now?" one of them asked.

Buzz smiled. "He's not lost," he said. "Not anymore."

After You Read

1 Match the sentence halves.

1 Forky jumped into the trash because he …

2 Bo Peep travelled from place to place because she …

3 Gabby Gabby wanted a new voice box because she …

a wanted to be a kid's toy.

b felt happy there.

c was a lost toy now.

2 Put the story into the correct order.

a Woody jumps out of the RV.

b Bonnie makes Forky.

c Woody begins a new life with Bo Peep.

d Gabby Gabby finds a new kid at the carnival.

e Bo Peep and Woody meet at the park.

f Woody gives Gabby Gabby his voicebox.

3 Answer the questions.

1 Which toy in the book is your favorite? Why?

2 What is your favorite part of the story? Why?

Glossary

antique (*noun*) something old that people sell and buy for money

backpack (*noun*) a bag that you wear on your back

carnival (*noun*) a place where you go to have fun; you can play games and win things and ride on a carousel

carousel (*noun*) at carnivals, people ride on the carousel for fun; it goes around and around and it usually has horses that are made of wood

crash past tense **crashed** (*verb*) to have an accident by hitting something; *He didn't want to crash.*

crayon (*noun*) children can use crayons to draw pictures with different colors

figure (*noun*) something, often a toy, that looks like a person

glue past tense **glued** (*verb*) to join things together with glue; *She glued some eyes on a plastic fork.*

GPS (*noun*) people use this in their car to tell them where to drive

kid (*noun*) a child

kindergarten (*noun*) a school for very young children

lamp (*noun*) something that gives light

lost (*adj.*) not knowing where you are; *Are you two lost?*

motorbike (*noun*) it looks like a bicycle but you drive it and it is very fast

RV (recreational vehicle) (*noun*) it looks like a large car; it has beds and a kitchen, and a family can drive it and stay in it on vacation

string (*noun*) it is made of threads of cotton and you can use it to hold things together

trash (*noun*) things that you throw away

voice (*noun*) the sounds that you make when you speak or sing

work past tense **worked** (*verb*) when something does what you want it to do; *I have one, too, but mine doesn't work.*

worried (*adj.*) unhappy or nervous about what is going to happen; *Bonnie was very quiet and Woody was worried about her.*

Play: Helping Others

Scene 1:

Bo and Woody are at the back of a carnival game. They talk to some toys on the prize wall.

TOY 1:	Hey! Can you help?
TOY 2:	We want to be prizes for kids. But the kids never win.
WOODY:	This game's too difficult. Not enough kids are winning toys.
BO:	Yep. We're going to change that!
WOODY:	How?
BO:	I'll show you. [Bo pulls a string on the game. She makes it easier to play.]

Scene 2:

A boy and a girl play the game.

GIRL:	[happy] I didn't win but ... I still won a toy!
BOY:	[happy] I won a toy, too!

Scene 3:

Bo and Woody watch the happy children with their new toys.

BO:	That's better!
WOODY:	The kids get a toy that they can love.
BO:	That's right. And the toys get the new home that they want.

Global Citizenship

Helping Homeless Pets

Sometimes pets need a new home—they're lost, or their owners are sick and can't care for them anymore, or they just don't want them. In most countries, there are organizations that find homes for dogs and cats. In London, the most famous of these is the *Battersea Dogs and Cats Home*. This home looks after about 7,000 animals every year.

The home helps to get lost pets back to their families. Some dogs and cats have no owners, and the home works to find good new homes for them. Possible owners can visit and see the animals, or they can see them online. The home brings together thousands of happy pets and families.

Animals can stay until they have a new home and family.

Find Out

Why is plastic a problem for the world?

People use plastic in many different ways, but plastic is also a big problem for the world. Most plastic becomes trash.

People often use plastic things once, then throw them away. This is called single-use plastic. In 2016, people bought one million plastic drink bottles every minute! Plastic bottles take 450 years to decompose.

A lot of plastic waste goes into the ocean. It's dangerous because the plastic breaks into very small pieces, called microplastics. Fish can eat the microplastics and die. This can also be dangerous for people who eat fish.

Plastic waste takes many years to decompose.

microplastics

Zero Waste Family

Bea Johnson is a writer who wants people to make less waste. Her family's waste for one whole year can go in a small jar! How do they do this? They are always thinking of new ways to make less waste and not use plastic. Here are some ideas:

- Use a metal water bottle.
- Always take your own bags to the store.
- Use forks and spoons that are made of metal or wood.

jar

decompose (*verb*) to break into smaller parts
million (*number*) the number 1,000,000
waste (*noun*) after you use a thing, waste is the part that you don't need and so you throw it away
zero (*number*) the number 0; if you take away 1 from 1, you have zero

Phonics

Say the sounds. Read the words.

oi

coin

voice

oy

boy

toy

Read, then say the poem to a friend.

A long time ago, when I was a boy
There were a lot of toys for me to enjoy.
But my favorite of all my toys
Was one for keeping all my coins.

A long time ago, when I was a girl
My favorite toy in all the world
Was not a doll with a lovely voice.
It was a toy for making a lot of noise!